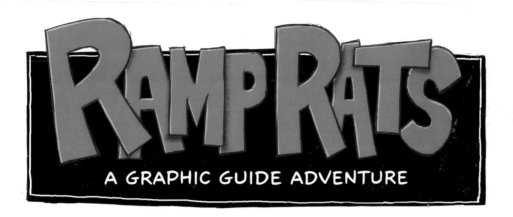

A GRAPHIC GUIDE ADVENTURE

WRITTEN BY
LIAM O'DONNELL

ILLUSTRATED BY
MIKE DEAS

ORCA BOOK PUBLISHERS

For Melanie, a master at Tony Hawk's Pro Skater and so much more. —LOD

Thanks to Jean-Luc Giroux for sharing his knowledge and trying to teach me a 50/50 grind. —MD

ACKNOWLEDGMENTS

Thanks to Marie Campbell for making these adventures a reality.

Library and Archives Canada Cataloguing in Publication

O'Donnell, Liam, 1970-
Ramp rats : a graphic guide adventure / written by Liam O'Donnell ;
illustrated by Mike Deas.

ISBN 978-1-55143-880-1

I. Deas, Michael, 1982- II. Title.

PN6733.O36R34 2008   j741.5'971   C2008-903028-1

First published in the United States, 2008

Library of Congress Control Number: 2008928577

Summary: Marcus spends the summer teaching his young cousin
to skateboard while bringing the local outlaw bikers to justice.

Disclaimer: This book is a work of fiction and is intended for entertainment purposes only. The author and/or publisher accepts no responsibility for misuse or misinterpretation of the information in this book.

Orca Book Publishers gratefully acknowledges the support for its publishing programs provided by the following agencies: the Government of Canada through the Book Publishing Industry Development Program and the Canada Council for the Arts, and the Province of British Columbia through the BC Arts Council and the Book Publishing Tax Credit.

Cover and interior artwork by Mike Deas
Cover layout by Teresa Bubela
Author photo by Melanie McBride • Illustrator photo by Ellen Ho

ORCA BOOK PUBLISHERS
PO Box 5626, STN. B
VICTORIA, BC CANADA
V8R 6S4

ORCA BOOK PUBLISHERS
PO Box 468
CUSTER, WA USA
98240-0468

www.orcabook.com
Printed and bound in China.
11 10 09 08 • 4 3 2 1

PEOPLE SAY GOOD SKATEBOARDERS ARE FEARLESS. IF THAT'S TRUE, THEN I'M DEFINITELY NOT A GOOD SKATER. MY GUT IS DOING BACKFLIPS AND MY HANDS WON'T STOP SWEATING, BUT IT'S NOT THAT MASSIVE LAUNCH RAMP THAT'S GOT ME SPOOKED.

YOU SURE YOU WANT TO DO THIS, BOUNCE?

NOT REALLY. BUT I CAN'T HIDE FOR THE WHOLE SUMMER.

JUST IGNORE CRUNCH AND HIS FRIENDS. FOCUS ON THE RAMP.

EASY TO SAY. HARD TO DO, PEMA.

HERE GOES DISASTER!

WENDELL "CRUNCH" REEVES AND HIS GOONS RULED THE SKATE PARK. THEY WEREN'T THE BEST SKATERS IN TOWN, BUT THEY WERE DEFINITELY THE MEANEST.

YOU KNOW THE RULES, BOUNCE. NO RODENTS IN MY SKATE PARK. GET LOST.

BITE COPING, BUTTBRAIN.

WHAT DID YOU SAY, LITTLE RAT?

N.. NOTHING..

PICK ON SOMEONE YOUR OWN SIZE, PIG-EARS!

FORGET IT, PEMA. YOU CAN HAVE YOUR SKATE PARK, CRUNCH.

PEMA'S OLDER SISTER NIMA TRIED TO MAKE US FEEL BETTER. SHE WAS A GREAT SKATER BUT HAD LOUSY TASTE IN FRIENDS.

WHY DO YOU HANG OUT WITH THAT JERK, NIMA?

THAT'S A JOKE, RIGHT?

HE'S NOT SO BAD ONCE YOU GET TO KNOW HIM.

I'LL WORK ON CRUNCH AND GET HIM TO LIGHTEN UP ON YOU, BOUNCE.

HE WON'T LISTEN. CRUNCH HAS BEEN A BULLY SINCE HE WAS SUCKING ON A SOOTHER.

WE HAVE TO DO SOMETHING ABOUT CRUNCH OR WE WON'T HAVE ANYWHERE TO SKATE THIS SUMMER. OUTSIDE THE SKATE PARK, THIS WHOLE TOWN IS A GIANT NO-SKATE ZONE.

PEMA HAD JUST MOVED TO HILLSIDE LAST YEAR, BUT SHE WAS RIGHT. FOR THE COPS, BUSTING SKATERS WAS A BIGGER SPORT THAN HOCKEY. WITH CRUNCH GUARDING THE PARK, PEMA AND I WERE MORE VULNERABLE THAN A ROOKIE IN OPEN ICE.

THERE'S NOTHING I CAN DO ABOUT CRUNCH. I'VE BEEN HIS FAVORITE PUNCHING BAG SINCE KINDERGARTEN.

YOU COULD TELL YOUR DAD ABOUT IT.

I HAVE! HE JUST TELLS ME TO BE A MAN AND STAND UP TO CRUNCH. EASY FOR HIM TO SAY. HE'S NEVER HAD TO FACE A BULLY AS MEAN AS CRUNCH.

HE HAS A POINT. YOU'VE GOT TO STAND UP TO CRUNCH SOMETIME. NO ONE ELSE CAN DO IT FOR YOU.

LAST TIME I TRIED THAT, CRUNCH REARRANGED MY FACE AND THREW MY SKATEBOARD IN THE LAKE.

CRUNCH ISN'T GOING TO LEAVE YOU ALONE. BESIDES, NEXT TIME YOU WON'T HAVE TO STAND UP TO HIM ALONE. I'LL BE THERE TOO.

YOU CAN PICK UP THE PIECES WHEN CRUNCH IS FINISHED WITH ME!

EVERY TIME CRUNCH BOOTED US FROM THE SKATE PARK, WE ENDED UP BACK AT THE SAME PLACE: SKATING IN FRONT OF MY DAD'S USED TRUCK LOT.

YOU SURE YOUR DAD DOESN'T MIND US SKATING HERE?

WHY WOULD HE MIND?

WATCH IT, KID!

BENNY, GET OFF THE ROAD!!

THAT'S WHY.

WHAT HAVE I TOLD YOU, SON? USE THAT BOARD IN THE SKATE PARK OR I'LL USE IT FOR FIREWOOD. GO GET CLEANED UP. YOUR MOM WILL BE BACK SOON.

ASHLEY AIN'T MY MOM.

START THAT STUFF AGAIN AND IT WON'T JUST BE YOUR SKATEBOARD I'LL USE FOR FIREWOOD.

TECHNICALLY, ASHLEY IS MY STEPMOM AND SHE'S NOT TOO BAD. I WAS JUST SICK OF BEING PUSHED AROUND, SO I WANTED TO PUSH BACK. BUT EVEN I KNEW WHEN TO DROP IT.

HERE SHE IS NOW WITH MARCUS. YOUR BROTHER IS OUR GUEST FOR THE SUMMER, SO MAKE HIM FEEL WELCOME.

HE'S NOT MY BRO — OKAY, OKAY. I'LL BE NICE.

REMEMBER BENNY IS ONLY TEN, MARCUS. TAKE IT EASY ON HIM THIS SUMMER, OKAY?

JUST AS LONG AS THE TWERP DOESN'T GET IN MY WAY.

I HADN'T SEEN ASHLEY'S SON, MARCUS, SINCE THE WEDDING THREE YEARS AGO. BACK THEN, HE WAS A GRUMPY KID WHO ATE TOFU AND TOLD MY DAD THAT HIS GAS-GUZZLING TRUCKS WERE DESTROYING THE PLANET. NOW THAT TAKES GUTS.

EVERY YEAR SINCE THE WEDDING, ASHLEY INVITED MARCUS TO LEAVE VANCOUVER AND SPEND THE SUMMER IN HILLSIDE, BUT HE ALWAYS SAID NO. DAD SAID HE WAS JUST A BIG CITY HIPSTER, TOO COOL TO HANG WITH US SMALL TOWN HICKS.

HERE LITTLE MAN, TAKE CARE OF THIS.

EVEN BIG CITY HIPSTERS CAN LEARN SOMETHING FROM US HICKS.

ALL TAKEN CARE OF, BIG MAN.

I LIKE YOUR STYLE, LITTLE BROTHER.

AFTER WE DRAGGED MARCUS'S BAG OUT OF THE ALLEY, PEMA AND I DISCOVERED MY STEPBROTHER HAD ONE THING IN COMMON WITH US: HE WAS A SKATER.

MOM SAYS THERE'S A NEW SKATE PARK DOWN BY THE LAKE. WE SHOULD CHECK IT OUT.

TOUCHY SUBJECT, MARCUS.

ZIP IT, PEMA.

OKAY, THEN LET'S SEE YOUR MOVES, BOUNCE. SHOW US A TRICK.

YEAH! SHOW MARCUS YOUR MASSIVE TIC-TAC MOVES, SKATERBOY!

ANYONE CAN TIC-TAC, PEMA!

FIRST, GET ROLLING ON A FLAT SURFACE. PUT YOUR BACK FOOT ON THE TAIL OF YOUR BOARD AND YOUR FRONT FOOT IN THE MIDDLE.

PRESS DOWN ON THE TAIL TO LIFT THE NOSE OF THE BOARD, AND TWIST YOUR HIPS. THE BOARD SHOULD FOLLOW.

BRING THE FRONT OF THE BOARD DOWN TO THE GROUND. THEN PRESS DOWN ON THE TAIL AGAIN.

THIS TIME, TWIST YOUR BODY TO THE RIGHT AND ROLL FORWARD.

JUST KEEP TIC-TACING LEFT AND RIGHT AND YOU'RE ROLLING.

BOUNCE, WATCH OUT FOR THE —

YAAAH!

— HILL.

THAT ALLEY BESIDE MY HOUSE HAD THE STEEPEST HILL IN TOWN. I LOVE RIDING MY BIKE DOWN IT, BUT I'D NEVER TRIED IT ON MY BOARD. I HAD NO IDEA IF I WOULD MAKE IT. GUESS I WAS ABOUT TO FIND OUT.

YAAAHH!

TOC!

AHHHH!

CRASH!

NOW YOU SEE WHY THEY CALL HIM BOUNCE.

AND HE TAUGHT US ANOTHER IMPORTANT LESSON IN SKATING: HOW TO CRASH!

CHAPTER 2
STREET SKATE BLUES

YOU SURE YOU WANT TO DO THIS. LET'S GO SWIMMING INSTEAD.

THE NEXT MORNING, MARCUS REALLY WANTED TO CHECK OUT THE LAKESHORE SKATE PARK. I TOLD HIM ALL ABOUT CRUNCH, BUT IT WAS NO USE.

YOU CAN'T AVOID THIS PLACE ALL SUMMER JUST BECAUSE OF A BULLY.

OH YES HE CAN. AVOIDING CRUNCH IS WHAT BOUNCE DOES BEST.

WHAT KIND OF NAME IS CRUNCH ANYWAY?

IT'S THE SOUND YOUR BONES MAKE WHEN HIS FISTS CONNECT WITH YOUR FACE.

CRUNCH-ALERT. STAY BACK, BOUNCE.

YOU TWO CAN COME IN, BUT THE RAT STAYS OUT.

IT'S A PUBLIC PARK. WE'RE ALL GOING IN.

YOU WANT THE RAT TO SKATE, YOU GO THROUGH ME.

THEN GET READY, 'CAUSE I'M COMING THROUGH.

WAIT!!

NO ONE HAS TO FIGHT. WE'LL SETTLE THIS AT THE LAKE JAM. IF MARCUS, PEMA OR I BEAT CRUNCH AT THE COMPETITION, THEN I GET TO SKATE HERE.

AND WHAT IF YOU LOSE?

IF WE LOSE, I CAN'T SKATE HERE EVER AGAIN.

DEAL. YOU GOT A WEEK TO GO FROM SKATE RAT TO SKATE KING. GOOD LUCK!

QUICK THINKING, BOUNCE. BUT CRUNCH IS A PRETTY GOOD SKATER. I DON'T THINK WE CAN BEAT HIM.

WITH MARCUS SKATING FOR US, WE MIGHT HAVE A CHANCE.

YOU CAN'T WIN A LAKE JAM WITHOUT A SKATEBOARD!

HEY!

MY BOARD! GIVE IT BACK, CRUNCH!

GO GET IT.

FIRST YOU NEED TO POP A BIG OLLIE. YOU KNOW HOW TO OLLIE, DON'T YOU?

OF COURSE I CAN OLLIE. HERE, I'LL SHOW YOU.

THE OLLIE IS THE MAIN BUILDING BLOCK OF MANY SKATING TRICKS. LEARNING HOW TO OLLIE IS THE FIRST STEP IN LEARNING HOW TO DO GRINDS AND KICKFLIPS AND TO PULL AIR OFF RAMPS.

FIRST, YOU GET ROLLING WITH YOUR BACK FOOT ON THE TAIL AND YOUR FRONT BETWEEN THE MIDDLE OF THE BOARD AND THE FRONT TRUCKS.

WITH YOUR BACK FOOT, SLAP THE TAIL DOWN HARD ON THE GROUND AND THEN JUMP INTO THE AIR AND FORWARD.

BEND YOUR KNEES AND PUSH YOUR FRONT FOOT TOWARD THE NOSE OF THE BOARD. THIS WILL BRING THE BOARD UP TO YOUR FEET AND LEVEL IT OFF.

USE YOUR FEET TO CONTROL THE BOARD WHEN YOU'RE IN THE AIR.

LAND THE BOARD ON ALL FOUR WHEELS AT THE SAME TIME AND BEND YOUR KNEES TO ABSORB THE IMPACT.

THEN RIDE AWAY IN STYLE!

NICE ONE. YOU'RE DEFINITELY READY TO SLAM A 50-50.

MY TURN. TALK ME THROUGH IT, MARCUS.

THE 50-50 GRIND IS ONE OF THE EASIEST GRINDS TO LEARN AND IT'S A GREAT TRICK TO IMPRESS YOUR FRIENDS. FIRST, APPROACH A LOW, SMOOTH EDGE LIKE A CURB OR A RAIL AT A MEDIUM SPEED.

AS YOU GET CLOSE TO THE LEDGE, POP AN OLLIE THAT'S HIGH ENOUGH TO GET YOUR BOARD ABOVE THE LEDGE.

LAND YOUR TRUCKS ON THE LEDGE AND LEAN BACK SLIGHTLY TO KEEP YOUR BOARD MOVING FORWARD. YOUR TRUCKS SHOULD SLIDE ALONG THE LEDGE AND YOU'RE GRINDING!

WHEN YOU FEEL YOURSELF SLOW DOWN, IT'S TIME TO GET OUT. POP ANOTHER OLLIE OFF AND TURN YOUR SHOULDERS TO DIRECT YOUR BOARD AWAY FROM THE LEDGE.

LAND IT, ROLL AWAY AND LISTEN TO THE ROAR OF THE CROWD.

NICE ONE!

WAY TO GO, PEMA!

DOUBLE CRAP.

EXTREME DOUBLE CRAP.

DON'T EVEN THINK OF RUNNING AWAY, BOUNCE. YOU KNOW YOU AIN'T SUPPOSED TO BE SKATING HERE.

HE KNOWS BOUNCE?

SMALL TOWN. OFFICER BRANCO KNOWS EVERYBODY.

YOU CAN EXPLAIN IT ALL TO YOUR DAD WHEN HE COMES TO THE STATION TO COLLECT YOUR SKATEBOARD.

YOU CAN'T TAKE HIS BOARD!

I CAN DO WHATEVER I WANT, KID. THIS IS MY TOWN. YOU GOT SOMETHING TO SAY ABOUT THAT?

HE DIDN'T DAMAGE YOUR CAR, AND NOBODY GOT HURT. IT WAS AN ACCIDENT.

AN ACCIDENT IN A NO SKATEBOARDING ZONE IS A CRIME IN THE EYES OF THE LAW.

YOU NEW HERE? YOU LOOK LIKE ASHLEY'S BOY. YOU GOT HER EYES. THAT'D MAKE YOU BOUNCE'S STEPBROTHER.

SO WHAT IF I AM? WHAT ARE YOU GOING TO DO ABOUT IT?

I WAS JUST GOING TO TAKE BENNY'S BOARD. BUT SINCE YOU'RE BEING SUCH A SMART GUY, LET'S ALL PAY A VISIT TO YOUR MOM. GET IN THE CAR.

BENEATH BRANCO'S POLICE BADGE BEAT THE HEART OF A BULLY. MARCUS MIGHT THINK HE WAS BEING BRAVE BY STANDING UP TO BRANCO, BUT LOOK WHERE IT LANDED US: IN THE BACK OF A COP CAR. MORE PROOF THAT STANDING UP TO A BULLY IS NEVER A GOOD IDEA.

CHAPTER 3
RAMP RATS ARE GO

YOU READY TO TELL CRUNCH TO STUFF IT, BOUNCE?

ARE YOU READY TO STITCH MY BODY BACK TOGETHER WHEN HE'S DONE WITH ME?

YOU'VE GOT TO STAND UP TO HIM SOME TIME. EVEN IF I BEAT HIM AT THE LAKE JAM, HE'LL JUST KEEP BUGGING YOU WHEN I'M GONE.

LIKE YOU CARE. YOU JUST WANT TO SKATE THERE SO YOU CAN HIT ON PEMA'S SISTER.

YOU LIKE NIMA? GROSS.

YEAH, NIMA'S PRETTY COOL. WHY DOES SHE HANG OUT WITH THOSE JERKS? DOES SHE HAVE A BOYFRIEND?

SHE LIKES SKATEBOARDING AND SO DO CRUNCH'S GOONS. AND NO, SHE DOESN'T HAVE A BOYFRIEND.

YOU GUYS PLAY YOUR DATING GAME AND SKATE IN THE PARK. I'M OUTTA HERE.

HOLD ON, BOUNCE. WE'RE NOT SKATING WITHOUT YOU.

BUT CRUNCH WILL ONLY LEAVE YOU ALONE WHEN YOU STAND UP TO HIM.

LIKE THAT'S EVER GOING TO HAPPEN!

IT'S GOT TO HAPPEN AND SOON, BOUNCE. WE'VE GOT TO SKATE SOMEWHERE OR NONE OF US WILL BEAT CRUNCH IN THE LAKE JAM.

YEAH, BUT WITH CRUNCH GUARDING THE PARK AND OFFICER BRANCO PROWLING THE STREETS, WE HAVE NOWHERE TO SHRED.

IT AIN'T MUCH. IF YOU CAN CLEAR IT, YOU CAN SKATE IT.

WE COULD BUILD A RAMP!

IT'D BE LIKE OUR OWN SKATE PARK.

IF IT MEANS YOU WON'T BOTHER MY CUSTOMERS, YOU CAN BUILD WHATEVER YOU WANT. DEAL?

DEAL!

NO SECURITY GUARDS TO HASSLE US.

NO CRUNCH TO BUST MY HEAD!

BY DINNERTIME, WE HAD MOST OF THE AREA CLEARED AND FOUND ENOUGH WOOD TO BUILD A PRETTY GOOD RAMP.

NICE WORK, GUYS.

TOMORROW WE'LL BUILD A RAMP.

CRUNCH BETTER WATCH OUT FOR THE RAMP RATS.

TAILSLIDES ARE PERFECT FOR LEDGES AND LOW RAILS LIKE THIS ONE. APPROACH THE RAIL AT A SLIGHT ANGLE WITH A GOOD BIT OF SPEED.

I'M FACING THE RAIL, SO THAT MAKES THIS TRICK A FRONTSIDE.

AND IF YOUR BACK WAS TO THE RAIL?

IT'D BE A BACKSIDE TRICK, EINSTEIN.

OLLIE UP AND OVER THE RAIL. TURN YOUR BODY 90 DEGREES AS YOU GO.

BRING YOUR BACK FOOT DOWN AND SLAP THE TAIL OF THE BOARD ON THE RAIL. YOU SHOULD START TO SLIDE.

AS YOU SLIDE, KEEP YOUR WEIGHT ON THE TAIL.

WHEN YOU START TO SLOW DOWN, TURN YOUR FRONT FOOT AND THE BOARD IN TO THE RAIL. YOUR WHEELS WILL STOP YOU SLIDING.

ALL YOU HAVE TO DO IS LAND IT.

AND SOAK UP THE APPLAUSE.

WAY TO GO, BIG BRO!

WHEN WE DROVE PEMA TO HER DAD'S BOOKSTORE, MARCUS WAS HOPING TO TALK TO NIMA. INSTEAD WE SPIED SOMEONE WE DEFINITELY DIDN'T WANT TO SEE.

IT'S THE HELL HOG BIKER!

WHAT'S HE DOING TALKING TO YOUR DAD?

NO IDEA.

THIS IS YOUR LAST WARNING. HAVE THE MONEY BY NEXT WEEK OR YOU'LL GET WHAT THE OTHERS GOT.

I'LL BE BACK NEXT WEEK, OLD MAN. YOU BETTER BE READY FOR ME.

PEMA WAS RIGHT. THAT GUY IS TROUBLE.

JUST LIKE OLLIES, GETTING AIR IS THE BUILDING BLOCK FOR MANY GREAT RAMP TRICKS.

THE NEXT COUPLE OF DAYS WERE PRETTY QUIET, IF YOU DON'T COUNT THE SOUND OF OUR HAMMERS BANGING TO FINISH OUR FUNBOX. PEMA'S DAD WOULDN'T TALK TO US ABOUT THE HELL HOG BIKER. WE HAD MORE IMPORTANT THINGS TO THINK

GET SOME SPEED, HIT THE RAMP AND STICK THE LANDING. THERE'S NOTHING TO IT.

IF IT'S SO EASY, WHY CAN'T I DO IT?

MAN! I'LL NEVER BE ABLE TO PULL IT OFF.

YOU ALMOST HAD IT, BOUNCE. YOU'RE TRYING TOO HARD TO GO BIG.

CONCENTRATE ON GETTING IT RIGHT. THEN YOU CAN WORK ON BLASTING IT BIG. TRY IT AGAIN AND I'LL TALK YOU THROUGH IT.

A FRONTSIDE GRAB IS A GREAT BASIC AIR TO LEARN. FIRST, YOU NEED SPEED. APPROACH THE RAMP WITH AS MUCH SPEED AS YOU CAN.

HIT THE RAMP WITH YOUR FEET IN THE POSITION TO OLLIE. BEND YOUR KNEES AND GET READY TO JUMP.

BLAST AN OLLIE JUST BEFORE YOUR BOARD REACHES THE EDGE OF THE RAMP. SLAP DOWN HARD ON THE TAIL, JUMP INTO THE AIR AND KEEP MOVING FORWARD.

AS YOUR OLLIE REACHES ITS PEAK, REACH DOWN WITH YOUR TRAILING HAND AND GRAB YOUR BOARD. BEND YOUR KNEES UNTIL YOU START TO COME DOWN.

AS YOU START TO DROP, LET GO OF THE BOARD AND LAND ON ALL FOUR WHEELS AT THE SAME TIME.

BEND YOUR KNEES TO ABSORB THE IMPACT OF LANDING.

AND THEN JUST ROLL AWAY.

YOU DID IT!

YOUR TURN, PEMA. SHOW BOUNCE HOW TO JUMP WITH STYLE.

ONE STALEFISH COMING UP.

A STALEFISH IS A BASIC AIR THAT LOOKS GREAT. IT'S ALL ABOUT CONTROL AND STYLE. ONCE YOU CAN LAND AN AIR FROM RAMP, YOU'RE READY TO TRY TO PULL A STALEFISH.

FIRST, APPROACH THE RAMP WITH A LOT OF SPEED AND GET READY TO PULL THE BIGGEST AIR YOU CAN.

ONCE YOU LAUNCH OFF THE RAMP, REACH WITH YOUR TRAILING HAND AND GRAB THE BOARD BEHIND AND BETWEEN YOUR LEGS.

NOW YOU'RE READY TO GO FOR STYLE POINTS. BRING YOUR KNEES FLAT AGAINST YOUR DECK AND HOLD IT AS YOU FLY THROUGH THE SKY.

AS YOU START TO LAND, LET GO OF THE BOARD, STRAIGHTEN YOUR LEGS AND GET READY FOR IMPACT.

BEND YOUR KNEES WHEN YOU LAND, KEEP ROLLING AND KEEP LOOKING GOOD!

NOW THAT'S A SERIOUS STALEFISH!

MARCUS WASTED NO TIME ASKING NIMA OUT. AFTER DINNER, HE WAS IN THE BATHROOM POSING AND PREENING IN FRONT OF THE MIRROR NEARLY AN HOUR. THEN HE WAS OUT THE DOOR WITHOUT A WORD.

PEMA WAS MORE ON THE BALL THAN I WAS. SHE GOT THEIR DATE DETAILS AND INSISTED WE FOLLOW THEM.

OKAY, I'VE SEEN ENOUGH. LET'S GO.

NO WAY! YOUR BROTHER DATING MY SISTER IS JUST TOO WEIRD TO MISS. KEEP QUIET OR THEY'LL SPOT US.

WE'RE NOT OLD ENOUGH TO SEE THEIR MOVIE. GUESS WE'LL HAVE TO WAIT OUTSIDE.

THERE'S CRUNCH! I'M NOT HANGING OUT HERE WITH HIM AROUND. LET'S SEE SOMETHING. ANYTHING! I DON'T CARE.

OKAY, BUT YOU'RE BUYING ME A JUMBO POPCORN!

LUCK MUST HAVE BEEN ON OUR SIDE. NOT ONLY DID I DODGE CRUNCH, BUT OUR MOVIE ENDED BEFORE MARCUS AND NIMA'S.

THERE THEY ARE. LET'S FOLLOW THEM.

ARE YOU SURE THIS IS A GOOD IDEA?

JUST KEEP QUIET AND THEY'LL NEVER KNOW WE'RE HERE.

THEY'RE JUST TALKING. THIS IS BORING. LET'S GO.

SHHH.

IT'S THE HELL HOG BIKER. WHAT'S HE DOING HERE?

MAYBE HE'S ON A DATE TOO.

CHAPTER 5
HOG HUNTING

BRING THAT SKATEBOARD BACK HERE, BOUNCE! I SAID NO MORE SKATEBOARDING, YOUNG MAN, AND I MEANT IT!

GETTING IN TROUBLE WITH THE POLICE TWICE IN ONE WEEK IS A GREAT WAY TO TICK OFF YOUR PARENTS. AND TO LOSE ALL SKATEBOARDING PRIVILEGES.

RUN!

YOU'RE CRAZY, BOUNCE. YOUR DAD WILL GROUND YOU FOREVER WHEN YOU GO HOME TONIGHT.

I'D RATHER BE GROUNDED THAN HAVE MARCUS'S PUNISHMENT.

YOU CAN SAY THAT AGAIN.

YOU CAN COME TO WORK WITH ME TODAY OR SIT IN A JAIL CELL WITH OFFICER BRANCO. YOUR CHOICE, MARCUS.

THIS SUCKS. THERE'S NO WAY I'M SITTING IN AN OPEN HOUSE WITH YOU ALL DAY.

YOUR STEPMOM IS REALLY TICKED ABOUT THE BROKEN WINDOW, ISN'T SHE?

SHE TOTALLY LOST IT WHEN SHE PICKED US UP FROM THE POLICE STATION LAST NIGHT. SHE BELIEVES BRANCO OVER ME OR MARCUS.

MY DAD KNEW WE HAD NOTHING TO DO WITH SMASHING THE WINDOW. HE SAID BRANCO IS A TRIGGER-HAPPY COWBOY.

SAME WITH MY DAD. HE COMPLETELY BELIEVED US.

ASHLEY IS CONVINCED MARCUS DID IT. SHE TOOK AWAY HIS BOARD, SO HE CAN'T SKATE IN THE LAKE JAM.

THEN WE WON'T BEAT CRUNCH. WHAT ARE YOU GOING TO DO?

WE'RE GOING TO FIND THE HELL HOG BIKER AND PROVE HE SMASHED THE WINDOW.

OH, IS THAT ALL?

SERIOUSLY, BOUNCE. EVEN IF WE DID FIND THAT BIKER, HE'LL NEVER TALK TO US. WE COULD TALK TO THE POLICE AGAIN AND TELL THEM WHAT WE SAW.

WE TRIED THAT LAST NIGHT. BRANCO WASN'T INTERESTED.

HE SAID WE WERE JUST MAKING UP THE RED TRUCK AND THE BIKER TO COVER FOR MARCUS.

I KNOW. I WAS THERE. REMEMBER? THEY MIGHT BELIEVE US NOW THOUGH.

THEY'LL BELIEVE US WHEN I SNAP A PHOTO OF THE BIKER AND HIS RED TRUCK.

A PHOTO ISN'T GOING TO PROVE ANYTHING! THERE ARE A MILLION RED TRUCKS IN THIS TOWN. AND JUST AS MANY BIKERS.

FINE. I'LL FIND HIM MYSELF.

HEY! COME BACK. I'M GOING TO HELP. I WAS JUST SAYING —

NEVER MIND.

WE CAN SKATE WHILE WE WAIT FOR HELL HOG BIKER. JUST WATCH OUT FOR BRANCO AND HIS BOYS. THEY'D LOVE TO CATCH US HERE.

YOU KEEP YOUR EYES PEELED AND I'LL SHOW YOU HOW TO NAIL YOUR KICKFLIPS.

KICKFLIPS ARE TRICKY TO MASTER. BUT THEY LOOK SO GOOD, THEY'RE DEFINITELY WORTH THE WORK.

GET ROLLING WITH A LITTLE SPEED AND YOUR FEET IN OLLIE POSITION.

PUT YOUR FRONT FOOT ON A SLANT, WITH YOUR HEEL HANGING OVER THE EDGE OF YOUR DECK.

SLAP DOWN A BIG OLLIE AND JUMP INTO THE AIR.

AS YOUR FRONT FOOT COMES FORWARD, SLIDE IT ACROSS AND FLICK THE EDGE OF THE DECK WITH YOUR TOES.

THE FLICK GETS THE BOARD SPINNING!

AFTER THE BOARD HAS SPUN 360 DEGREES, CATCH IT WITH YOUR FEET AND LAND THAT SUCKER.

GET YOUR FEET OVER THE BOLTS, BEND YOUR KNEES AND REMIND YOUR FRIENDS THAT YOU KICK BUTT!

YOUR TURN ON BIKER WATCH. WATCH THIS HEELFLIP.

HEELFLIP? COOL. LET'S SEE IT.

HEELFLIPS ARE JUST LIKE KICKFLIPS, EXCEPT YOU FLIP THE BOARD WITH YOUR HEEL. GET ROLLING ON FLAT GROUND OR JUST IN FRONT OF A LEDGE.

GET YOUR FEET INTO OLLIE POSITION.

PUT YOUR FRONT FOOT JUST BEFORE THE FRONT TRUCKS AND HANG YOUR TOES OVER THE EDGE OF YOUR BOARD.

SLAP DOWN ON THE TAIL AND JUMP INTO A BIG OLLIE

AS YOUR FRONT FOOT COMES FORWARD, SLIDE IT OUT AND KICK THE EDGE OF THE DECK WITH YOUR HEEL.

GET YOUR LEGS OUT OF THE WAY TO LET THE BOARD SPIN UNDER YOU.

WHEN THE BOARD HAS SPUN 360 DEGREES, CATCH IT WITH YOUR FEET AND LAND.

KEEP YOUR FEET OVER THE BOLTS, BEND YOUR KNEES AND ROLL AWAY IN STYLE.

WE SPENT THE REST OF THE MORNING LOOKING FOR THE HELL HOG BIKER, WITH NO SUCCESS. WE HEADED BACK TO MY PLACE FOR LUNCH, AND THAT'S WHEN OUR LUCK CHANGED.

THE HELL HOG IS TALKING TO YOUR DAD!

THIS DOESN'T LOOK GOOD.

I DON'T NEED YOUR SO-CALLED PROTECTION. YOU AND YOUR BOYS CAN RIDE YOUR BIKES INTO THE LAKE FOR ALL I CARE.

YOU'LL REGRET THIS, HANK. IT'D BE A SHAME TO SEE ALL THESE NEW TRUCKS GO UP IN FLAMES.

THAT'S THE GUY WHO SMASHED THE WINDOWS LAST NIGHT!

AND THREATENED MY DAD.

HE'S THREATENED A LOT OF PEOPLE AND SMASHED A LOT OF WINDOWS.

HE'S THE VANDAL OFFICER BRANCO IS LOOKING FOR. AND I'VE BEEN PROTECTING HIM FOR FAR TOO LONG.

CHAPTER 6

RAMP RATS BITE BACK

AS LONG AS WE PAID, WE WERE PROTECTED.

AND IF YOU DIDN'T PAY OR TALKED TO THE COPS, THEY'D COME AND SMASH YOUR WINDOWS.

IT'S NEVER GOOD TO FIND OUT THAT YOUR DAD HAS BEEN PROTECTING CRIMINALS. NOT THAT HE HAD MUCH CHOICE. FOR THE PAST YEAR, THE HELL HOG BIKERS HAD BEEN DEMANDING PROTECTION MONEY FROM ALL THE BUSINESSES IN TOWN.

THAT'S WHY THE BIKER WAS HARASSING MY DAD!

THE HELL HOGS ARE A BUNCH OF BULLIES, LIKE CRUNCH AND HIS GOONS.

WHY DIDN'T YOU STAND UP TO THE BIKERS, LIKE YOU'RE ALWAYS TELLING ME TO DO WITH CRUNCH?

I GUESS IT'S EASIER TO TALK ABOUT STANDING UP THAN IT IS TO DO THE ACTUAL STANDING.

BUT NOW THAT MARCUS IS GETTING THE BLAME, THE BIKERS MUST BE STOPPED. I'M NOT PAYING THEM ANOTHER DOLLAR.

IF YOU DON'T PAY, THEY'LL COME BACK, WON'T THEY?

YUP. AND I'LL BE WAITING FOR THEM.

GOOD. BECAUSE I HAVE A PLAN TO CATCH THESE BIKERS.

DAD WASN'T CRAZY ABOUT MY IDEA, BUT HE DIDN'T HAVE ANYTHING BETTER. WHEN THE SUN WENT DOWN, WE GOT STARTED.

ARE YOU IN POSITION? GOOD. STAY THERE. ASHLEY WOULD SMASH MY WINDOWS IF SHE KNEW YOU KIDS WERE HERE TONIGHT.

GOOD THING SHE'S GOT A LATE HOUSE-VIEWING TONIGHT. AND DON'T WORRY, WE'LL STAY OUT OF SIGHT.

WE'VE GOT A GREAT VIEW FROM HERE. MARCUS AND NIMA, ARE YOU IN POSITION?

ON MY WAY THERE NOW.

I CALLED THE POLICE STATION FROM THE HOUSE PHONE. THE CHIEF SAID THAT OFFICER BRANCO IS ON HIS WAY.

GET READY. HERE COME THE HELL HOGS.

WHERE YOU GOING?

TO GET THAT CAMERA BACK!

PLEASE TELL ME WE'RE NOT RACING THEM TO THE BOTTOM OF THE HILL.

OKAY, I WON'T. BUT WE ARE.

THEY HAVE TO FOLLOW THE ROAD. BUT WE CAN MAKE OUR OWN.

AND DODGE GARBAGE AS WE GO! THANKS FOR ANOTHER FUN DATE, MARCUS.

WE MISSED THEM.

NEXT CROSSING FOR SURE. WE'VE GOT TO SKATE FASTER.

FASTER?!

IF I GO ANY FASTER, I'M GOING TO END UP STUCK TO A DUMPSTER.

ME TOO, BUT WE GOTTA CATCH THOSE BIKERS.

WHAT WE NEED IS SLIDE CONTROL.

POWER SLIDES ARE THE ONLY BRAKES A SKATER HAS. THEY COME IN VERY HANDY WHEN YOU NEED TO SLOW DOWN IN A HURRY.

FIRST, GET YOUR FEET OVER THE TRUCKS ON YOUR BOARD.

WITH MOST OF YOUR WEIGHT ON YOUR FRONT FOOT, DRAG YOUR BACK FOOT AROUND 90 DEGREES, SO THAT YOU'RE FACING INTO THE HILL.

KEEP SOME WEIGHT ON YOUR BACK FOOT SO THAT THE BOARD SLIDES ON THE GROUND.

ONCE YOU ARE SLIDING, LEAN BACK TO KEEP IT GOING.

WHEN YOU'VE SLOWED ENOUGH, SLIDE YOUR BACK FOOT BEHIND YOU TO GET THE BOARD ROLLING AGAIN.

NOW, LET'S CATCH UP TO MARCUS.

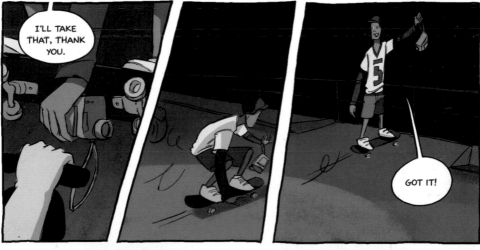

CRASH!

CHAPTER 7
CRUNCH TIME

I'M SUNK. I'LL NEVER BEAT CRUNCH WITHOUT MARCUS.

THE REST OF THE NIGHT WAS A BLUR OF YELLING COPS AND SCREECHING FIRE TRUCKS. BY THE TIME THE LAKE JAM KICKED OFF THE NEXT MORNING, MARCUS WAS STILL IN THE HOSPITAL AND CRUNCH WAS SKATING LIKE A PRO.

IT'S NOT ABOUT BEATING HIM, BOUNCE. IT'S ABOUT STANDING UP TO HIM.

SHE'S RIGHT, YOU KNOW.

MARCUS! YOU MADE IT! WHERE'S YOUR BOARD?

IT'S GONNA BE HARD TO SKATE WITH THIS THING ON.

IT'S UP TO YOU, BOUNCE. ONLY YOU CAN SHOW CRUNCH THAT YOU WON'T BE CHASED FROM THIS SKATE PARK.

LIKE THAT'S GOING TO HAPPEN. THOSE BANKS LOOK PRETTY BIG. I DOUBT I CAN GET ENOUGH SPEED TO REACH THE COPING.

THE TRANSITIONS FROM BOTTOM TO TOP ARE STEEPER THAN THE ONES ON OUR RAMP.

YOU'LL HAVE TO LEARN HOW TO PUMP YOUR WAY UP TO THE LIP, BOUNCE. C'MON, I'LL SHOW YOU HOW IT'S DONE.

WHETHER YOU'RE RIDING BOWLS, MINI-RAMPS OR HALF-PIPES, KNOWING HOW TO PUMP ON THE TRANSITION IS KEY TO GETTING TO THE COPING AND PULLING TRICKS.

FIRST, GET SOME SPEED AND RIDE TOWARD THE TRANSITION.

WHEN YOU REACH AS FAR AS YOU CAN GO UP THE TRANSITION, STAND UP STRAIGHT AND GET READY TO ROLL BACK DOWN.

AS YOU ROLL DOWN, BEND YOUR KNEES AND PUT YOUR WEIGHT FORWARD. THIS WILL PUSH YOU DOWN THE TRANSITION.

ROLL THROUGH THE FLAT BOTTOM AND INTO THE OPPOSITE TRANSITION. WHEN YOU GET AS HIGH AS YOU CAN GO, STAND UP AGAIN AND GET READY TO ROLL BACK.

I WENT HIGHER THIS TIME!

AS YOU ROLL DOWN THE TRANSITION, BEND YOUR KNEES AND LEAN FORWARD AGAIN. TIME IT RIGHT AND YOU'LL GET MORE SPEED AND GO HIGHER ON THE RAMP EACH TIME.

COOL, I'LL HIT THE LIP THIS TIME FOR SURE.

MADE IT!

GOT THE TRANSITIONS NAILED?

YEP. I MIGHT ACTUALLY HAVE A CHANCE NOW, THANKS TO NIMA.

READY FOR MORE GOOD NEWS? THE POLICE CHIEF WATCHED THAT VIDEO YOU SHOT LAST NIGHT. THEY ARRESTED THOSE HELL HOG BIKERS AND CHARGED OFFICER BRANCO WITH TAKING BRIBES.

SCORE ONE FOR THE SKATERS!

AND OUR NEXT SKATER IS BENNY "BOUNCE" SHARP.

YOU'RE UP, LITTLE BRO. REMEMBER, FOCUS ON YOUR SKATING AND COMMIT TO THE TRICKS.

DON'T WORRY ABOUT WINNING. JUST SKATE HARD AND HAVE FUN OUT THERE.

I DROPPED IN AND EVERYONE CHEERED. WELL, ALMOST EVERYONE. CRUNCH AND HIS BUDDIES LAUGHED AND SHOUTED STUFF AT ME. NO SURPRISE THERE, I GUESS.

AS I SPED TO THE FIRST RAIL, CRUNCH'S LAUGHTER ECHOED IN MY MIND. BUT THE SCREECH OF MY TRUCKS GRINDING AGAINST THE METAL DROWNED IT ALL OUT.

WITH EVERY AIR I BLASTED AND KICKFLIP I LANDED, THE FEAR THAT HAD STALKED ME FADED AWAY.

SOON, IT WAS JUST ME, MY BOARD AND THE TRICKS OUT THERE. I HAD NO FEAR OF FALLING. I WASN'T SCARED OF BAILING. AND I WASN'T SCARED OF CRUNCH.

WHEN MY RUN WAS OVER, I KNEW WHAT I HAD TO DO.

LET'S HEAR IT FOR BENNY "BOUNCE" SHARP!

WAY TO GO, BOUNCE!

WENDELL "CRUNCH" REEVES
BENNY "BOUNCE" SHARP   88.5
ERIC LION   81.5
PHILL "IT UP" PAULSON   80.0
JUSTIN "PARADISE" PAULSON   76.0
FRANCES "FRANKIE" ALLEN   70.5
BEN OBERSTEIN   63.5
MIKE "CORNWALL" CORNWALL   30.0
                                     20.5

SWEET RUN, BOUNCE!

IMPRESSIVE, SON.

YOU REALLY ROCKED IT, BOUNCE.

BUT I DIDN'T BEAT CRUNCH.

THAT'S RIGHT, RAT. AND YOU KNOW WHAT THAT MEANS. GO BACK TO YOUR STUPID RAMP AND DON'T EVER COME TO MY SKATE PARK AGAIN. GOT IT?

WATCH YOUR MOUTH OR I'LL —

IT'S OKAY, DAD. I CAN HANDLE THIS. CRUNCH AND I HAD A DEAL.

IT WAS A BAD DEAL, BUT I KNOW HOW TO MAKE IT BETTER.

GIVE ME BACK MY BOARD!

GO GET IT!

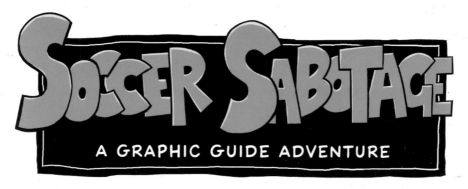

ABOUT THE AUTHOR

FROM CHAPTER BOOKS TO COMIC STRIPS, **LIAM O'DONNELL** WRITES FICTION AND NON-FICTION FOR YOUNG READERS. HE IS THE AUTHOR OF THE AWARD-WINNING SERIES "MAX FINDER MYSTERY." LIAM LIVES IN TORONTO, ONTARIO.

ABOUT THE ILLUSTRATOR

MIKE DEAS IS A TALENTED ILLUSTRATOR IN A NUMBER OF DIFFERENT GENRES. HE GRADUATED FROM CAPILANO COLLEGE'S COMMERCIAL ANIMATION PROGRAM AND HAS WORKED AS A GAME DEVELOPER. MIKE LIVES IN VICTORIA, BRITISH COLUMBIA.